"Helena has done it again. It's about time this book came out! Fresh and original perceptions! If you are ready to have the author and her divine team ignite your imagination with the unique, insightful considerations of inter-dimensional perceptions of the reality of true Celestial Beings... then pick up this book and get comfortable. It's quite a compelling read to pause and give contemplation to. This book will have you put your chin in your hand and go hmm, fascinating."

—*Zale Zeviar, Spiritual Teacher, Author, and Businessman*

"This book uses a down-to-earth, yet well-defined language, full of guidance and insights. I truly enjoyed reading it and am planning on coming back to it a few more times."

—*B. Lee, Spiritual Student*

"This somewhat futuristically themed book compelled me to expect the unexpected. I found it interesting and surprising at times. Introduced concepts expanded my mind and my beliefs."

—*Alex Jirek, Computer Specialist*

"I met Helena at a book reading event. She read this line from her mini-book *WAKE UP! Your Heart Is Calling*: 'Your heart has its own intelligence. The heart's intelligence is superior to that of your mind'. That was enough to get my attention to her work. I bought that book immediately. In reading her book *Evolution*, I found myself captured at the poetic style of writing. I quickly felt as if I were reading a book by Nostradamus. This intrigue kept me engaged, as I read sometimes amusing, yet always awakening messages. That our civilization is ready to evolve, that we are getting new bodies, time is non-existent, time is for those who can only do one thing at a time. This last line of how we have limited ourselves really stuck in my mind. I am grateful for these teachings. I'm truly looking forward to reading more from the series!"

—*Lydia Olechny, Astrologist*

EVOLUTION

It Is Time for the New You

Purposeful Mind Series – Book Four

Other Books by Helena Kalivoda

AWAKEN!
Your Soul Is Calling

WAKE UP!
Your Heart Is Calling

WAKE UP!
Prosperity Is Calling

Purposeful Mind Series:

CREATION
Accessing Your Untapped Potential

ILLUMINATION
Getting to Know the Invisible You

CONTEMPLATION
Understanding Your Inner World

EVOLUTION
It Is Time for the New You

METAMORPHOSIS
What Else Is Possible?

EVOLUTION

It Is Time for the New You

Purposeful Mind Series – Book Four

HELENA KALIVODA

AUDRENAR BOOKS

EVOLUTION
It Is Time for the New You
Purposeful Mind Series – Book Four

Copyright ©2014 by Helena Kalivoda
Published by Audrenar Books

Library and Archives Canada Cataloguing in Publication

Kalivoda, Helena,
Evolution / Helena Kalivoda.

Poems.
ISBN 978-0-9877521-3-0

I. Title.

PS8621.A469E96 2012 C811'.6 C2012-902411-2

Editing: Agnes L. Kirby
Cover art: original oil painting by Jaroslav Kalivoda

For more information on this book and other books by Helena Kalivoda visit www.booksbyhelena.ca.

*I am dedicating this series to my family
and to all who are searching to reconnect
with that part of Divinity we call Self.*

CONTENTS

CONSCIOUSNESS

11

ACKNOWLEDGEMENT

I am grateful to my Higher Self for her continued support. My sincere thank-you goes to Agnes L. Kirby for her kind and unwavering help editing this series of *Purposeful Mind* books.

I appreciate my family for their support of my writing. Thank you all, my incarnate and spiritual muses, for your presence in my life.

Helena Kalivoda

PREFACE

Evolution is the fourth of five books in the *Purposeful Mind* series. It contains themes of Time, discourses about The Earth, The Universe, our future New Bodies and more.

In regards to the verses referring to the Earth's evolution, some of them may feel intimidating or worrisome. The main message is to remember that we, being the creators we are, have a full say in which way our destiny will unfold. Will we become obsolete through our material greed and relentless exploitation of our planet? Will we rejuvenate our Mother Earth and ourselves and become a race of joyful, caring beings? Only we can answer these questions to ourselves. Nobody else can direct and set our destinies.

I have been receiving guidance from the Spirit world for over fifteen years and it has been a time of profound awakening for me. I wish for you to deepen your awakening process when reading and contemplating on this series.

Helena Kalivoda

TIME

THE TIME KEEPERS

We, The Time Keepers, we know all.
We record those deeds of yours.
We do not judge, as otherwise,
we would be judging ourselves.

We can tally all that you need to know.
We can tally your previous lives.
We can tell you your future patterns.
We can lead you today.
What do you say?

We are building trust between you and us.
We are helping you to understand who you are,
and through that, we understand who we are.
We are The Time Keepers from times bygone.

The Time Keepers are those
who are moving in many different realms.
The Time Keepers are those
who are not concerned with time,
as the past, the present and the future are now.

Time, as you know it,
is not time, as we know it.
Time, as you know it,
does not exist in our realm.
Time, as you know it,
is a linear tick-tock,
is an element that you don't quite understand.

What we are keeping are the eons,

philosophical turns, centuries of philosophy,
centuries of thoughts that gel plots into reality,
centuries of events of different cultures
in thought patterns.
That is time, as we comprehend it.

To us, time is an element wherein all adds up
and a different era appears.
A new era,
a combustion of the thoughts into plots
that ripen and happen,
and are what you experience
in your time.

BUT WHAT IS TIME?

Time is a variable of yours and ours.
Ours is about a span unknown to you.
Your time is bemusing you
to the point of you feeling
that you are not having
enough of that which you call time.

But what is time?
Time is just the splitting of your life
into a new parcel, so you can say,
well, yesterday I was here,
tomorrow I will be there.

How does it translate where we are?
It does not. We don't have linear time.
We are multidimensional beings
that are in charge of time,
the variable that is perceived by you
as lasting eons and eons of your time.

These eons can be a blink of an eye.
These eons can be a blink
that brings new analogies, new theories,
new worlds and new catastrophes.

Just remember, yours is a tick-tock,
ours is times of transitioning
to a new era of thoughts and philosophy.
And that is a way
to differentiate your and our time.

SEE THROUGH THIS GAME

Beware of the pitfall
that time bequests on you all.
Time, where we are,
is of no importance at all.

You can span time
to visit and see places
that are far away.

You can propel yourself to places
that one can imagine.

You can propel yourself to places
that one can see,
if one is not bound by time.

Please see through this game
of time controlling what you do,
as you cannot be free
with time pulling you.

Pulling you toward the abyss
of forgetting who you are,
as you cannot see
that your Thee is timeless
and is without time.

Time is your ally seemingly,
but not so, as you are willingly
forgetting, because of time.

The lesson is,
please be aware of the abyss
that time creates.

Time can be your ally
if you know that really
time does not exist.

TIME IS FOR LINEAR THINKERS

You can be unaware of who you are
and that you can stop time.
How do you do that?

You can be keen on stopping time.
Just like yesterday, when you said,
I don't know why,
but I am totally immersed in this cooking,
and nobody cares if I am looking
totally worn out,
if time is speeding and I cannot,
I cannot keep up with the demand.

So how did you stop time?
You engaged others to help
and time stretched.

Hmm, you say, are you humouring me?
Oh yes, why not, we are a humorous lot,
but now, seriously.

Time is for linear thinkers.
Time is for linear happenings.
Time is for those who, at most,
can manage only one thing at a time.

And who are those who work under this premise?
Are they all who live on this trellis,
the trellis of your galaxy?
Are others inhibited by time?

Not quite so severely.
But certain hampering must be used,
until all will not misuse
the way of congealing their thoughts
into reality.

Once you understand
that your thoughts create,
you will be better equipped
to work with time without time.

Let's imagine there is no time.
All is flat and unwavering.
Life is not at all boring,
as it is spanning through millennia.
Time is a variable that is not.

That is the time that beckons us.
That is the time we experience.
That is how we live, how we are.
We are who we are every time
we think the thought that creates us.

THE TIME KEEPERS ARE HERE

Mais oui, mais oui, here we go again.
We are entering your thought train.
We are entities from afar,
we are The Time Keepers, yes we are.

We are The Time Keepers of eons of time
that is different from the time
you experience on your planet.

Our time is not the time you know.
Our time is a destiny put into perspective.
Our time is time that cannot
be measured by your clock.

Our time is an important link to you,
as it is measuring
your evolutionary position within,
your position of understanding who you are.

We, The Time Keepers,
are floating through millennia.
We, The Time Keepers,
are of a different modality,
as we are entrusted with knowing
when to enter another reality
to help the process of evolving.

The aspect that we call time
are the times that exist
as evolutionary parameters.

We are The Time Keepers
who measure the evolutionary process.
We are The Time Keepers
who measure the life of your planet
in evolutionary times
and not in time as it is known to you.

BECOMING ONE

The Time Keepers are here and are ready to leave
after the message is brought to you:

Your time has come.
It is your time to move on,
to take the evolutionary step,
to listen to your heart instead of your head,
to become one.
To become one with all around you,
with all of those who are on the same path,
who are as ready as you.

Please keep clear your vision
of yourself who is one,
as that is a catalyst to all that will come,
that will come to embalm your planet.

You are one.
One, with us and yourself,
and all dimensions.
There is no separation.
All is one.

We are here to make it clear,
oneness is a state of mind.
Oneness is a state of becoming one
with yourself and the rest,
that is becoming one with itself
and you.

THAT PRIMORDIAL MASS

Here we come again
to tell you to have a good day.
We are travelers through time.

We zip from place to place.
We are not here to stay,
we come and go.
It is not play. It is our role.

We are The Time Keepers.
We are The Watchers of Time.
We are The Time Keepers from so near,
yet so far.

Time is a variable that does not exist.
Time is of value on the Earth
where time is a nice way of saying,
here, have it all in the linear way.

Our time is different.
It is not linear.
In our time, all happens at once.

And what does it mean, you say.

It is as this, and pardon us,
if we do not make too much sense.
Abracadabra it ain't,
so here it comes.

There was time such as ours everywhere.
There was time like this a long time ago.

There was an absolute quiet and dark.
There was a primordial mass
that was going nowhere.

That mass woke up and started to bubble.
That mass created different worlds.
That mass created continents on the Earth.

That mass is the Universe
and it continues to grow.
That mass, and have no objection,
that mass is also you and me.

That mass is an omnipotent, everlasting creation.
That mass is what is called God.
That mass is a critical component—
that mass is that which creates all of us.

Who created that mass?
Well, God.
Do you see the interaction?
If not, here it comes:
That mass called God was God to start with—
that mass started as God.

Who, then, started that mass?
God did, and He is that mass.
What this really means is (and you are getting it)
that there is no beginning and no end.
There is not and never will be.

Hard to understand?

Do you know why? Because you are
a promoter of linear thinking.

Do you see what we mean?
If not, because you are a linear thinker.
That is not to say you are worse or better.
Remember? You are that mass!

With this thought, we leave you and go away again.
Don't worry, call us up by our name.
Say, Time Keepers, Time Keepers,
please do come again.

TIME AND SPACE

Perplexing are the earthly differences of times.

Times are changes of atmospheric pressure,
changes such as migrating
from one country to another.
And times are just time,
such as keeping time
by knowing the day's hours.

That is not what the Universe perceives.
It is not what it believes.
The belief system on Earth is so vastly different
that the Universe sometimes cannot comprehend
what humans' needs are.

It sees you traveling from an office to your home.
It sees you discarding, like a little gnome,
your routines for other routines,
all for the sake of time.
There does not seem to be enough
of this non-existent time.

Hmm, hmm, non-existent, you say.
But how is it, if I may say,
that it does not exist?
As we are continuing to keep it,
as we are defeated by it
and are affected by it?

Time is a way of categorizing the events
so they appear linear to you.

Time and space, two different propositions.
Time influences space,
and time is influenced by space.
What a novel way of saying,
I live in space, therefore I am driven by time.

IMAGINE YOUR DAY LONG

This discourse is on the demands of time.
Is time a variable that does not exist?

Hmm, you say, how is it possible?
How is it that we have clocks
and we, in flocks,
are hurrying in all directions?
We are creatures that live by time.
We are creatures that need time.
Without time, the day is not possible.

The day is not possible,
as that is what you think.
The day is not possible,
as that is what you imagine.
However, a day is a stretchy thing.
You can make your day to be long or short.
You can make your day to be what you want.
The day is yours to stretch, as you want.

Hmm, you say, how do I do that?
How do I stretch my day?

We will say, just do it.
To imagine is a very trendy
thing to do today.
Imagine your day long,
and it will stretch.

Oh, well, you may say,
why should I be the one

to jump on the bandwagon of imagining?

Imagination seems to be a way
to fix all aches,
to correct all problems,
to mess all up and then unravel it,
to sing the blues and then put gaiety back in.

What you imagine will transpire.
What you imagine will be your lot.
So sit back, enjoy your imagination,
enjoy your relaxation.

Have a picture of what you desire,
relax, and keep that picture
in your mind for some time.
Then let it go and be sure
that this picture will endure
on its own and will become
what you want.

You can stretch your day
by imagining
that the day you want to stretch
is stretched already.
And then sit back and enjoy your long day.

THE MEASURE CALLED ETERNITY

All is well.
It is as well as it could be,
as all is counting and clicking,
all is continuing as it should be.

Continuity at your place
is adhered to by using time.
Here, we are not using time.
We are using the measure called eternity.

No time, no pain, no electricity.
No beat to the working drum.
No helpless yelping,
no accusations or jealousy.

No fighting, no electrocution,
no admiration.
No nothing, it seems.
No nothing, it is.

FREE YOURSELF FROM TIME

We move here, and let's make it very clear,
we move here very effortlessly.
We do not depend on your time measurements.
We do not depend on your clock.
We are free from space, and eternity is the place
where we live and progress.

If you understand what it means,
you may get a glimpse of our reality.
What you need to do,
and this may sound somewhat simple and crude,
is to become one that does not keep time.[1]

If you live like that
you will plant the seed that will breed
your inner independence from time.

Can you live like that? Oh, certainly you can.
You can train your thoughts
to behave differently.
You can do what comes naturally.

If you wish,
we will be with you to help you
if you need to go to one of your meetings,
meetings that can be wasteful and not too eventful,
that can be a great waste of time,
a great waste of time that does not exist.

---

[1] The author listened to the advice and stopped wearing her watch while being employed, and was never late for her numerous meetings.

Free yourself from that non-existent time
and prepare yourself to experience
your timeless, space-less origins.

You can have these experiences if you imagine
that you are a being who is a Soul,
and you do not limit yourself
by the oppression of time and space,
for you can travel timelessly to visit the Universe,
to experience that time does not exist.

THE EARTH

THE EARTH WILL NOT BECOME EXTINCT

Your life,
as it unfolds before and all around you,
may disappear into forgetfulness,
as this so-called planet Earth, your nest,
will go through upheavals and changes.

During the Earth crisis,
the Earth will move to reveal
her new age in a squeal of a moment
that will be here.

The Earth will not become extinct.
The Earth will not be shaken that badly.
The Earth will be creative and will recover,
and madly
will fall in love with the people again.

These people will be a noble breed.
These people will understand nature.
These people will be of a fine mould,
a mould of godly thoughts and deeds.

These people are here already today.
Some of them are ready,
some are just awakening.

THE EARTH IS THINKING

The Earth is heaving
and is working toward her freedom.
The Earth is malnourished and is sad.
This woman is not well and is singing the blues.
She is empowering herself from her snooze
to the realization that she, the Earth,
has been submissive,
has not been owning her power,
this woman that it is not.

And so, the Earth is thinking,
well, this is not working.
I will change my ways,
as I am the power
and will exhibit who I am.

I have the power to change my destiny.
I have the power and I will.
I have the power,
and I will not submit myself anymore
to the treatment that is dished on me by people,
by the race I took to my bosom.

The Earth decides to undo what was done to her.
The Earth decides to undo the years of abuse
and will tear herself from the noose
that is encircling the globe
and will not be submissive any more.

ALL IS CHANGING

Your planet may be getting ready
to shed her coat.
Some people could be better off
it they owned a boat.

A boat that is big and strong,
to survive the times that are here—
deluge, snow, floods, earthquakes,
small fires, big eruptions,
all possible earthly shakes,
and earth crust corruptions.

Nature is beautiful, omnipotent.
Nature is kind,
but at times, needs to unwind
when she feels that the meal
dished to her by humanity
is poisonous and indigestible,
unhealthy for humans
and Earth alike.

All is flexing. All is changing.
Humanity's consciousness is rising.
The new times are here.
A new era of humanity,
a new era for the planet is here.

CREATE A REALITY YOU WILL LIKE

You are your reality maker,
as you are changing your probable future
every second of your existence.
You are the one who creates
what you live.

How and who is changing the day?
It is you and you, and you...
You, by your dedication
to the routine of living life your own way,
the non-supportive or supportive way.

Is apocalypse coming?
It is as near as you allow it to be.
Who are we to say that it is or not,
as you are creators of your own lot.
You create your destiny
that you may enjoy or not.

But then, if you can perceive
that the change that is coming
has been of your own doing,
you may decide to create a reality
to your liking.

MOTHER EARTH IS GIVING

The morning is unfolding
and it will be a beautiful day.
A day of pleasures and excitements,
sorrows and horrors, joys and armaments.

A day of all experiences,
experiences across the globe.
The globe that nurtures and loves you,
and is called Mother Earth.

Mother Earth, mother,
as in someone who loves you,
as in someone who nurtures you,
as in someone who gives and gives.

Mother Earth is giving, is very giving
to the last drop of her blood.

I NEED A DOCTOR

Blue sky, isn't it?

Oh, yes, very, very blue.
Oh, it is not anymore.
Why?

It is polluted. It is not clean.
The air is thick and it is hard to breathe.
The air is not clean.
The Earth has problems breathing.

The Earth has congested lungs.
The Earth is coughing and saying,
I need a doctor.
I need oxygen.
I need a pump to clear my lungs.
I will call the cosmic wind to clear it,
I will call the wind of change to move in
to clear the congestion in my lungs.

Cancer-like substances
are weakening her structure.
Cancer-like substances
are decomposing her nature.
Enough, you Earthlings,
clean your own house.

And if you will not,
the Earth will clear herself
from what you gave her
as a reward for caring for you.

The Earth will clear you as well—
she will do a good weeding of you.

Some will stay on
as they are a new breed of people.
Some of you will be smitten
and left to realize
that the ways you employed
cannot continue.

The chain is as strong as the weakest link,
and the chain is not strong today.
Therefore, Mother Earth will have to have her way,
unless you realize that you are in charge
and start behaving in ways
that strengthen every link
between you, Mother Earth,
and the Universe.

HUMANITY, BE READY

The Earth is getting ready for the time
when you all understand
her role as a mother to you,
who nurses you.

Do not worry about your status.
Do not worry about your prestige.
Any cataclysm will make a mockery
of earthly priorities
that are not based on living from the heart
and spirituality.

Pestilence, hunger, resonance of thunder,
all these may be coming to you—
pestilence, hunger, and resonance of thunder.

Pestilence is a way of perceiving God
as being angry and naughty.
Isn't that the thought?

Perhaps we need to say it again—
you are the ones playing the game,
you are the ones who are in charge,
you are the ones who are preparing your own
stash,
stash of unhappiness or happiness.

YOU CAN STOP THE EARTH TREMBLES

Are the Earth changes a fallacy?
This all depends on you.
You, who are living on this Earth.

Can you comprehend?
You are the makers of your Universe.
You are the influencers and creators.
You can move mountains
and you can stop the Earth trembles.

Earth changes? Are they coming or not?
The planet is not too well.
The planet Earth is in need of help.
The planet Earth is calling to you.
A lot, a lot depends on you.

By understanding your needs,
you will understand Earth's needs.
By balancing your life
you will balance Earth's life.

All is one and one is all,
and no one, no one lives
by herself on a lonely atoll.

THE AGE OF WOMAN

Elements are rising.
There will be an uprising,
an uprising in the fundamental core beliefs.

The Earth is getting ready
to do a little twist and shake-about
to get rid of those who are not,
not ready to turn around
and embrace the new thinking.

A new way of living from the heart.
A new way of thinking
that is changing the core beliefs
of those who will see it come.

It will come as a lion, roaring and fighting.
It will come as a pussycat.
It all depends on your point of view.
It depends on you.
Are you ready to start a new journey?

A new journey that is inevitable.
A new journey that is already in full swing,
as you all are on the verge or the brink,
the brink of the new era called
The Age of Woman.

It is an age of new ideas and plots
that do not include wars
and other toys liked by those
who are now called men.

Feminine energy is rising.
It is here to take care of the planet.
It is here to implement a new wisdom—
an ageless wisdom—from Gods and Goddesses
of this Universe.

THE UNIVERSE

YOU AS A PRIMORDIAL MASS

The Universe is the old master.
The Universe is not a procrastinator,
the Universe does not procrastinate.
The Universe is living,
the Universe has its own body.
The Universe.

The Universe is a multidimensional beast,
a multidimensional feast
of all and nothing,
of small and big,
of reliable and not,
of beautiful and menacing,
of all that is surging, throbbing,
churning, melting,
and is always in motion
in a primordial soup-like state,
in a primordial mass of elements
that are building, rebuilding, tearing,
planning, playing, squirming,
that are moving in all directions,
that are constantly thrown together and apart,
that are sacred and are not.

Understand?
All, all is a part of the Universe—
good, bad, evil, godly.
Mesmerized by this thought?
Mesmerized by the thought of a stew
that is always on its way to a new,
a very newest happening?

You, as a primordial mass,
you were also the squirming thing
that was not so pretty as you think.
You were a little squirming mass
that was not ready to pass
any tests
until it developed into a prettier picture
of guidance, of prosperity,
of those things that are valued,
that are a gift of God,
that are a gift.

That squirming little thing
evolved into a beautiful person.
That squirming thing called protoplasm,
is not so proto any more.
It is a triumphant conglomeration of that
which is given by God
and it recognizes beauty,
recognizes its own will,
recognizes its own role,
recognizes its own life needs,
recognizes its own—its
own maladies and pleasures,
own degrading and upgrading,
own multidimensional nature,
own meditative state,
own primordial urges,
own manifestation of love.

YOU ARE ON THE BRINK OF DISCOVERY

You are on the brink of discovering
your roots, your God, your center,
your Jehovah, Christ, Buddha,
and all that you came to call yours.

Exciting times are coming—
the new understanding
that is seeping into minds of the people.

The new understanding
of the Universal primordial matter
flowing to every nook and cranny
to uphold the world.

The world that is not static, that is not solid.
The world that is always changing,
that is created and recreated
at all times.

The world that is beautiful,
that knows itself,
that has all the knowledge
of God, of her way.

Say:
I know that I am what I am.
I am God's child.
I am her child, who is who she is.
Amen.

THE UNIVERSE SAYS, WHAT IS IT?

Mais oui, mais oui, all we can say
the Universe is not child's play,
although childlike qualities
are to be beheld.

It is not child's play,
as the Universe is a serious game,
where angels, archangels, and all the saints
are playing a billiard game.
Oh, well, excuse our cosmic joke...

The Universe is vast and peaceful
if that is what you believe.
It is mad and chaotic
if that is your belief.

The Universe is asking, what is it?
Is it warm or cold?
Is it changeable or is it stable?
Is it peaceful or at war?
Is it one or the other?

You decide!
Do you see the pattern?
You are a creator, you are a decider,
you are the omen, you are.

AUM WAS THE WORD

The Universe is the Universal truth.
The Universe is the call of Gods and Goddesses.
The Universe is.
The worlds in the Universe are vast and small—
as people are short and tall.

The Universe was created millennia ago
by an energy called God.
God, as the Universal Creator,
decided, as he was omnipotent and alone,
that worlds were needed
and the worlds would be his playground.

He created all by the power of thought,
and Aum was the word.

THE UNIVERSE IS HOME TO ALL

The Universe is round, flat, square,
all possible shapes together.
The Universe is an omnipresent entity.
The Universe is a full circle of life,
just as your birth, puberty,
adulthood, and death.
Then it starts again.

The Universe is where you are,
whether you are 'dead' or 'alive'.
The Universe is, always was, and will be.
The Universe is a large complex body
that houses anybody
who is part of the Universe—
stars, macabre beings,
humans, and all other neat things.
The Universe is home to all.

THE CYCLICAL NATURE OF THE UNIVERSE

Inevitable Earth changes
are coming to change the Earth.
Or is it the Earth that is changing herself?

Consider the question
about the chicken and the egg.
Which came first?

Well, it will not affect the outcome
if one would say none!
All is true. None is true.
Why?

One is affecting the other.
All is the beginning and the end.
The beginning is the end,
the end is the beginning.

The cyclical nature of the Universe
is the Creator's idea.

If it was created by Him,
who created 'Him'?
Do you follow what I mean?

If not, oh well,
the time will come when you will.
And you can bet that will happen soon,
and then, in a moon, all changes again.

OPEN YOURSELF TO THE UNIVERSE

Elementary Watson, elementary.
All is new, if considered new.
All is old, if considered old.
All is absolutely as you say.
All is absolutely as you pray.

If you pray for forgiveness, you will get that.
If you pray for comatose, well, you will be.

If you cannot understand that you, as a creator,
you are the one to take a stand,
then you cannot behave as you desire,
because you yourself are full of contradictions
and need to acquire jurisdiction
over yourself, over your mind.

What you need is to open your mind
to the world above, to the Universe.
The Universe is the mother of all,
and after all, you are a mother too.
You want your children to respect you,
love you, and cherish you.

Think of the stars, think of the mass,
the primordial mass
that is still brewing and spewing life
into the Universe,
and open yourself to that Universe.

Think of that mass that is you,
that is a girl grown up into a woman
who is sitting and writing this,
after you opened yourself to the Universal forces,
millennia ago and today.

YOUR BODY

YOUR BODY WILL BE MADE ANEW

To achieve the extraordinary,
elevate yourself above the mundane.
Elevate yourself to bring changes
to yourself and others.
Elevate yourself.

The Gods are ready for a turnover
and you are as ready as you can be.
There is not too much to do
in terms of changing destiny.

Will you be able to live on?
To live on with your earthly bodies,
bodies that are not divine,
bodies which decay and rot?

Hmm, that actually is another plot.
If you wish, and know how,
your bodies can be made anew.

Your bodies would be indestructible,
if you just knew how to guide them.
If you just knew how to caress them.
If you just knew how to take care of them
so they can take you into a new world
where bodies are imperishable
and live forever.

This is the past and this is the present.
The future is the same
and bodies can remain.

It is you who will acquire
this new skill of maintaining your body,
for millennia to come.

It is up to you to make your body
anew,
a new way of experiencing
your godliness.

This is not of the future.
It has been done by others before,
and shall also be done by you
once you remember that you too
are Divine.

THE BODY WILL EVOLVE

Humanity is a testing ground,
and you all can be so proud.
It is a testing ground for a future step.

The body will evolve to be taken with you.
The body will be taken to stay.
The body will be used
again and again.

This means that after that day,
procreation will become a thing of the past
that will be remembered
and then forgotten at last.

That time is coming.
Your body will become one with your Soul.
Your body will not burn or rot.
Your body will not be embalmed or put into soil.
Your body will live forever.

Forever, as a statement of your eternity.
As a statement of the truth, to embody.
The truth that was revealed by Jesus,
when he became one with his body.

Jesus, who left with his body forever
when he suffered an earthly fate
and was hanged as a criminal.

Jesus, who wept the bitter tears of pain,
bore the inhumane trial

and called from a wooden cross
for his Father.

His Father, who seemed to forget him,
who knew that it was not up to Him,
God, but up to Jesus to discover the truth,
the truth that you will discover soon.

YOUR BODY WILL BECOME LIGHTER

Get up and take a stand.

Get up and be ready to belong
to those who are steady, ever so steady,
crossing over to meet us,
crossing over to greet us
with their fully grown bodies.

Bodies that are not of ether.
Bodies that are of matter,
that is lighter and must be taken care of
in a different way than before.

Body that is lighter and not so dense.
That does not need food
and in that sense
is not the matter you got to know.

Exciting times are coming.
Exciting times are near.
Meditate and invite
your eternal body and eternal Spirit
to combine into one.

Please meditate tonight,
on your body that is changing.
Body that is being regenerated,
and it also can be cleansed
by your own thoughts.

You are near a revelation
that you are in the position
of entering the Kingdom of God
with all you have, your body intact.

BE THAT ICARUS

You are the dust from the stars.
You are the dust of consciousness.
You are your own destiny maker
and you are near a breakthrough.

A breakthrough that took millennia to make.
A breakthrough that almost sounds like
you can eat and also keep your cake,
as you can be of all worlds—
earthly, and the others.

All is said. You are a grad
of the school called life.
A grad, who is ever ready
to step out and take flight,
the flight of a chance.

Be that Icarus[2],
don't worry about burning your wings.
Be a star,
as you actually are made of stardust
that got encrusted.

You are made of stardust.
Your return is a must.
The congealed form must go.

---

[2] From Greek Mythology, the son of Daedalus, who flew, using his wings made from wax and feathers. He was too close to the sun and the sun melted the wax. The wings fell apart and Icarus fell into the sea and drowned.

The matter make-up must move
and make room
for a different and new form,
a new form of reality
that will come to pass
in this millennium.

A NEW MATERIAL BODY

Your body belongs to you.
Your body is not apart from you.
Your body grew with you
and is yours.

Your body is becoming an experiment.
What happens next
is that you will be able
to take your body with you.

And you may say,
why would I like to do such a thing?
I could be in a blink wherever I want to,
and a body is heavy and cumbersome,
and a body is so, so cumbersome.

Well, it is not so. This body of yours
will undergo a change.
It will undergo ionization
that will give it a lighter dimension.

This body will be more ethereal
and of lighter material.

It will be disposable in a sense
that you will understand
that you are not that body
and that you can leave it
and come back at your will.

Dilemma comes when the body says:
That's it, I am tired, I don't want to live forever.
Thus, the body must undergo changes,
changes on material and spiritual levels.

Accumulation of debris from previous lives
will be discarded.
Radical changes will be so slow
that very few will notice or know.

TELEPATHY WILL PREVAIL

As a human being,
you are accustomed to names.
Names are not of significance,
they will not be anymore.

Discarded will be the human voice.
Words will be no more.
Telepathy will become
your means of communication
above all.

New times are coming.
You will be called upon
to live in an era of understanding
that you, as a human being,
are first of all
Divine.

THE BODY IS LIFTED BY THE SOUL

Jesus was born to show
there is a Soul that is free.
The Soul is in you and is your Thee.
There is a free Spirit
that is not encumbered by a body.

Contrary to that,
the body is lifted by the Soul.
The body can be purified and cleansed
by the Soul's presence
and can be taken with you.

Your body is a jumble if you let it be one.
Your body can be pure and beautiful
if you take care of it,
and it will be with you many lifetimes
if you can prepare it
to last that long.

The question is, why?
Why would you want your body
to come with you?
Isn't it something
that needs to be discarded?
Isn't it a shell that is left behind?

It is and it is not,
as this shell is a durable one.
Its purpose is evolving.
This shell will serve you
and will do the following:

it will be your safety net
when you will be prepared
to leave this planet
and move to another dimension.

Another dimension is being worked on
by angels and archangels.
It is being prepared
to receive you and your brethren,
all those who are ready
and are rising steadily to understand
that the third, physical dimension
will undergo a big change.

It will 'split' into several:
the old third dimension,
the elevated third,
and that which is not yet
fully known.

YOUR BODY NEEDS TO TRANSFORM

'Derelicts' are coming home.
They are prodigal daughters and sons
who lost their homing tone,
who are not knowingly staying where they are,
who are the ones who need to be told
that the Earth has no hold.
The Earth has no hold over them
if they decide to return home.

How do you return home?
In your body? In your mind?
In your Earthly naked garb
of bones and flesh,
or in some other kind?

Your body will transform.
Transform into a less material one
that is light and less dense,
is less corruptible,
and, in a sense, is a new body
based on the old body
which came to be improved.

You know, like in 'new and improved?'
Oh, well, just a little cosmic joke
about your new and improved products!

Your body is on its way
to becoming a filmier, lighter body.
And you ask, what does it mean?

Will I be able not to feel queer
while I am here on the Earth?
How will I look and feel?
What will people see?
A freak or a Saint?
Or will they be able to sense
any difference?

You still will look like a human
but you will also look like somewhat more.
You will look like one who still has acumen
on Earth but also in Heaven.
You will be clear in how you think.
You will be more decisive.
You will be more of a mediator
than a fighter.

New gear? New body?
Who ever heard of that?
Whoever will believe that it may happen?

It is an illuminating thought.
It is an illumination from God
that is omnipotent and reachable.
Reachable from your thoughts,
reachable from the indescribable joys
in all your hearts—
mental, material, emotional, and spiritual.

THE UTERUS

Your uterus is on strike
as it feels it will not be needed any more.
It is a part of your old system
that is undergoing a change
toward your new body.

Your uterus knows this and it is upset.
This is not what it likes to see—
you and your Thee
working on changing your body,
as it is preparing to ascend.

Your uterus is saying,
well, these two are playing
and I cannot not exist.
I must be, I must.
Let's do some trick,
let's do what they notice,
let's be sick.

Let's be sick and also miserable
so they will know that I matter.
When they see that I matter,
they will pay attention to me.

Hark, hark, laugh the other organs,
what is going on in here?
What is it, what is it?
We want to hear
this news about
a uterus-less body.

Who thinks that such body is complete?
Who thinks that such body is not a defeat?
Who thinks that it is the way it should be?

Let's go on strike, let's show them
that we are together,
that we are a group.
That we are a group of organs
that nobody can regroup
into a different body.

Hmm, hmm coughs another organ,
I am important as well.
I serve as a carousel
that takes you in and out.
That's right, I am your heart
that beats one, two, one, two.

All organs on alert!
Someone wants to take a mallet
and beat us to a pulp,
so we don't matter anymore.

Hmm, hmm,
come on you organs, come on.
None is after you, you are all important.
Yes, you are, even you amazing uterus.

Is this what you can say,
is this what you can see,
is this you, wonderful Thee,
is this so?

Yes, it is, and this is the plan.
All I can say is that not one organ
will be diminished in its service.
Not one will be entitled to retirement.

We are all needed,
is that what you say?
Is this a game? Is this a play?

No, it is not. There is no plot.
Uterus as an organ will prevail
and it will help to lift the big veil,
the veil that covers the other side
of the things to come—
such as the bliss that brings you home,
such as a realization
that you are not that little after all,
that you are a powerful creator
who, by herself, can change the world.

Your uterus will participate
in bringing bliss into yourself
from the loins upwards
to your zone of understanding
who you are.

YOUR BODY IS YOUR FRIEND

Your body is your shield.
Your body is your friend.
Your body is an object that you need
to better comprehend.

Your body functions as you let it.
If you are sad, your body is not glad
as it is forced to produce poisonous material
that can clog the arteries
and also harm your heart.
Being sad is an emotion
and is not a motion,
so it will linger as sediment.

If you are happy, your body knows.
Your body can become a joyous,
very joyous receptacle for your Soul
when the Soul is not surprised
by an oppressive onslaught,
but is allowed to sing and is never sad.

Alas, the same goes for crying.
If you stifle it, it creates a problem.
It creates sediment
and so on.

Your body is as healthy as you allow.
Your body is as healthy as it can be.
You are the one that is dictating the rules.
You are the one that is not or is helping
by deciding your moods.

BE NICE TO YOUR BODY

Do not be lulled into a belief
that the body is just grief.
Your body is an important messenger
of you to others and of others to you.

It is a body that delivers a message
when you cry or shout with joy.
It is a body that delivers all—
that is, when you live on the planet Earth.

Therefore, be actively pursuing
a body that is not sick, but that is well
and does not have a spell
over you.

It is constantly pulling for you
to defend you and cover you,
to hug you and love you.

It can only do this if you reciprocate.
It can only cast that spell on you
if you cast your spell on it.
It is a simple rule of the Universe.

The body is a shell carrying you forward,
so carry your body well.
Be nice and pleasant with your body.
Do not belittle its figure,
keep it well.

THE BODY IS AN INSTRUMENT OF LOVE

Love your body fully.
Love your body with all your might.
Take care of your body.
Do not partake in anything
your body does not like.

Your body is an instrument of love.
Your body is a fine instrument
that needs to be used with respect,
that needs to be used to open the ways
to perceive the joy and power of love.

Your body has several gates.
Your body can attune to the higher spheres.
Your body will evolve to be taken with you.
Your body is not as destructible as you may think.
Your body can be rearranged to fit,
to fit the high purpose of life—love.

CONSCIOUSNESS

THE FEMALE ENERGY IS HERE

The times are changing and the time is near.
The female energy is here
to alleviate the world's troubles,
bring the wisdom of the sages
and populate the Earth with those
who, at least and at most,
understand who they are.

The current times are near the end.
The heart is the one that will play
a role in the evolution of the people,
of those who are ready to usher in
the new age.

As the new age is ushered in,
it will need, as any age before,
the support of those who can help it
to become evermore
a reality.

Blessed are those who can hear the guidance.
Blessed are those who are ready and prepared,
as this is the time when all are called
to deliver their dream the best they can.

This dream is a dream that is becoming.
It is not just a dream any more.

TAKE THE STEPS NOW

You forgot where you came from.
You forgot that you took on another form
to experience another level of reality
and bring your experiences
back to your original home.

These coming times will be an eye opener.
These coming times' development
will be focused on your Soul,
not on the earthly, on the material.

You can take the steps now.
You can start discovering who you are.
You can talk to others on the subject.
You can write your thoughts down,
or you can just live your lives
as honestly and simply as you can.

Be honest to yourself every minute of your life—
honest about your feelings,
honest about what you really believe,
honest about the way you speak,
honest about every breath you breathe.

Take the steps now.
Prepare yourself to live
in these extraordinary times.

TAKE THAT FIRST STEP

Why don't you relax?
Put your feet up?
Why don't you cuddle yourself
in your arms?

Why don't you perceive
the passing of time
between your fingers
that are gentle and smooth,
that can smooth wrinkles
from your tired blues,
smooth out your discord and disharmony,
smooth the wrinkles away.

Don't listen to the cacophony,
the cacophony of time.
Beat on your own drum.

It is time to let go.
It is time to get up,
as this is the time of coming home,
coming home to be with us,
with us who are helping and hoping
to welcome you and embrace you
in our eternal arms.

What does it take, you ask.

Well, you know it all.
You know what you need to do.

You know that all is a part
of you taking a step forward.

Your step is your next move.
A step that is not measured.
A step that is a voluntary act.

Your first step is as follows:

Be curt? No.
Be happy? Yes.
Be miserable? No.
Be kind? Yes.
Be quiet? Kind of.
Be explicit? Why not.
Be yourself? Sure.
Be adorable? Absolutely.
Be perceptive? Yes.

All these qualities you possess,
if you want.

Relax, take a breath.
Your dreams will not come true
if you will not take that first step.

MEDITATE ON YOUR OWN POWERS

Illuminating, as it may be,
you are on the threshold of a discovery,
discovery of who you are.
Open your eyes wide to see the Light
that is within and is shining bright.

Do not search around you,
you are not within if you are always without.
Abolish the thoughts
that are not helping and are at odds
with who you really are.

You came to follow your destiny.
Your destiny is the destiny of a warrior
who will find his armour
broken and will be vulnerable
until he understands that armour from without
is not as strong as the armour from within.

Meditate on your powers
to realize what they are
then follow up on a message
that tells you who you are.

Exercise your power to the point
that you will be joined with all around
and then you will hear very clearly
the messages that abound.
About infinity, about God,
as this is what you came to find out
this lifetime around.

HUMANITY, WAKE UP

All is done. Now is the time to act.
Obliterate your thoughts
of sorrow and sadness.
Obliterate your thoughts
of jealousy and smallness.

All-healing love is present in you.
All-healing love flows around you.
It combines with others' healing love
and embraces all
that swim in an ocean of love.

Humanity, wake up.
You are entering a new era.
You are conquering yourself.
Your milestones are coming close.
Your milestones, when embraced,
will change the face of the whole Universe,
not just yours.

Wake up. Wake up the blue planet.
Wake up the planet and take a quantum leap.
You are ready to step out,
to reach out, to transform yourself.

Your people are asking, finding, and releasing.
Your people are ready. The planet is ready.

Let's shake off the chains of old thought patterns.
Let's smile, joyfully living happy,
mesmerizingly happy thoughts.

Be ready to encounter your Higher Selves.
Be ready to declare:

I am a Universal being
of the vast, vast Universe,
of the vast, vast pool of Souls,
of the primordial mass,
of the Consciousness that is so vast
that is spanning ad infinitum.

YOURS TO DISCOVER

You are working to achieve en masse
what others have previously achieved one by one.

They achieved a state of enlightenment
but the masses did not wake,
did not wake up from their daze
or break free from their earthly haze.

How do I do it, you may ask.
That is the task of your discovery.
You discover. That is yours to do.
We cannot explain something
that is not due. The words are short,
the vocabulary is not available,
the description is not pure.

That is why you need to experience
all the steps to bring you to the point
where you just simply know.

It is a result of your doing.
It is a result of faith in yourself,
faith in your accomplishments
and your love, your all-embracing love
that, as a dove, is soaring high
to spread its wings and cover the Earth.

CULTIVATE A FINER YOU

Be your own lighthouse of Light.
Be your own lighthouse.

Do cultivate a finer you.
Do cultivate a body
full of strength and grace,
a mind that is not hard
but is as gentle as
a butterfly's wing
brushing against your face,
that is lighter than a fingertip's flutter,
that is lighter than a whisper of time.

HOMECOMING

Humanity is
stardust turned human,
stardust that is ancient and filmy,
stardust that is vibrating ever so softly,
stardust that is, was, and will be.

Humanity is a congealed consciousness
that has turned as thick as molasses.
Humanity is the material end of things.
Humanity is on the verge of discovery.

Stop and listen to the bells—
they toll not of death.
They toll and are full of joy.

You are on the way to discovery.
You are on the way to the recovery
of your joy and happiness,
of your all-encompassing lovely presence
that graces all.

Homecoming is the highlight of your journey.
Homecoming is your ticket to ride.
You can and you will,
after you restore your belief
in yourself.

WE WILL BE INSEPARABLE

I am your Higher Self.
I am here by myself
and I am waiting for you
to come and join me.

When this moment comes to pass,
you and I will really grasp
what this partnership means.
We will be inseparable.
We will be one and so close,
so close that we will never be torn apart.

The day will come
when all will follow the cosmic plan—
a plan of evolution, the blueprint
that will be known and therefore,
will be the one that will be followed by all.

REACH BLISS

The mesmerizing effect of daily meditation
will be repeatedly imprinted on your brain,
will be able to train you to reach bliss.

Bliss that you can have
when you let your heart play
a leading role in your evolution.

Open your heart,
your bridge between the physical
and Spirit.

Open your heart, your bridge
to a world based on love and truth,
a world that will make all feel alive
with unconditional love,
with intuition,
with Light.

SULKING OR GAIETY?

Mais oui, mais oui, here we come again.
We come to interrupt your thought train,
a thought train that is a runaway truck
that is galloping and speeding away.

How are you doing today?
Are you as happy as you would like to be?
If not, what it is that is not allowing you to be
a happy, an immensely happy person?

Why don't you master your thoughts,
as they are 'things' that can change your lot.
What is it going to be?
Sulking or gaiety?

You are the decision maker, or are you not?
What is it going to be?

It will be a glory day when all realize
that you are not your thoughts.
That you are not of flesh,
that you are an ageless
Soul.

JOYFUL AND CLEAR

During your sojourn, you will meet many Souls.
You will be engaged in many toils.
You will be accepted by some
and rejected by others.
You will carve your niche by helping your brothers.

All unhappy feelings and cravings will cease.
You will qualify for a respite from greed,
for an unimaginable feeling of love and peace.

You will acquire skills,
skills that will take you
on the next step of your journey
through times and spaces,
throughout centuries that do not exist.

Experience the godliness within you,
of you and others.
Lead a life that is joyful and clear,
that is full of meaning,
so you can glean the Universal truths.

WHAT IS IT GOING TO BE?

This is what it is,
you may or may not believe it.
You are the maker of your universe.
You are the maker of your own fate.
If you are not welcome, so to speak,
it is because you never wanted to be
invited in the first place.

What is it going to be?
Are you or are you not?
That is the question.
Are you or are you not the one
to believe in yourself?
Are you or are you not the one
to believe in your own potential?
Are you or are you not the one
to believe in your own progression?

Answer those questions you pose to yourself,
then be ready to accept the answers.
What is it going to be?
You and your Higher Self are asking you,
what is it going to be?

Will you understand?
Will you be the one to lead yourself?
Will you be the one to accept
that you are a star, a shining star,
which has fallen from Heaven to Earth?

THIS DAY IS SIGNIFICANT

The Universe is not the one to interfere.
It loves you, it wishes you all the best
on your long, long quest
of remembering who you are.

The Universe loves you and asks you
not to be afraid of what you are—
beings from the stars.

Star beings who are the ones
who can understand
that they are the stars,
that the dinosaurs did not die.

Star beings who are aware
that the whole world is a picture of ideas
that are processed in the Cosmos
by beings who are starry,
by beings who never worry
about their existence and are fully engaged
in their world of passion with the spiritual.

The day of remembering is significant.
It is a day when you conquer yourself.
This day is noteworthy as you realize
that you are a being that is reaching for the sky,
that you are a being who is free.

WITHIN YOU

All is well. The rest is to come.
The rest, as in your guidance from above.
The rest, as in your connection to your Higher Self
whereby you transform your forceful nature
and become a creature
of peace and calm.

There is a dwelling of wisdom,
calm and peace,
that is within you.
There is a shrine
that needs to be discovered.

Please do meditate and be calm.
Please do meditate and seek
those who, like you, are a part
of a movement to usher in
the new times.

To usher in the new times,
to sweep out the debris
of human belligerence.

Listen to your heart.
Your heart is telling you
that you are not a creature
that is only flesh and physical matter.

ABOUT THE AUTHOR

Helena Kalivoda is an award-winning author devoted to sharing inspirational messages that support readers in transforming their lives. Lives of peace and happiness can be available to those who learn the power of creation through an open heart as encouraged by Helena's books.

AWAKEN! Spirit Is Calling, Helena's first book, contains powerful truths for each person's journey. These poignant teachings were downloaded from Helena's spirit guides. Be prepared for your 'aha' moments when reading the book.

Her second book, *WAKE UP! Your Heart Is Calling,* leads readers to realize that all aspects of humanity, when denied pure love, are bound to eventually fail and cannot be healthy. This book connects to an online environment where you can access extended resources to help you apply the learned principles.

WAKE UP! Prosperity Is Calling, Helena's third book, outlines The Seven Principles to Living a Life of Prosperity. These principles will become your truth and experience once you use them and live them consistently.

Currently, Helena is working on a new series of *Purposeful Mind* books of poetry. This book, *Evolution,* is the fourth book of this series.

Helena holds a BA in Economics and B.Sc. in Computer Science. She is a mother of three, living in Canada. In 1997, she left the corporate world to continue the writing she started in the early nineties.

Visit www.booksbyhelena.com for more information about Helena Kalivoda's books.

www.ingramcontent.com/pod-product-compliance
Lightning Source LLC
LaVergne TN
LVHW091200080426
835509LV00006B/765